The Bringer Discourses

On Waking Up to the Mind Control Programs of the Matrix Reality

The Bringer Discourses

On Waking up to the Mind Control Programs of the Matrix Reality

S. F. Howe

Diamond Star Press
LOS ANGELES

The Bringer Discourses: On Waking Up to the Mind Control Programs of the Matrix Reality

Copyright © 2020 S. F. Howe

Published by Diamond Star Press
Trade Paperback: First Edition
ISBN 13: 978-1-7324591-2-0
ISBN 10: 1-73245-912-6

Books by S. F. Howe

Matrix Man
How To Become Enlightened, Happy And Free In An Illusion World

The Top Ten Myths Of Enlightenment
Exposing The Truth About Spiritual Enlightenment That Will Set You Free!

The Bringer Discourses
On Waking Up To The Mind Control Programs Of The Matrix Reality

Secrets Of The Plant Whisperer
How To Care For, Connect, And Communicate With Your House Plants

Vision Board Success
How To Get Everything You Want With Vision Boards

Sex Yoga
The 7 Easy Steps To A Mind-Blowing Kundalini Awakening!

Transgender America
Spirit, Identity And The Emergence Of The Third Gender

Morning Routine For Night Owls
How To Supercharge Your Day With A Gentle Yet
Powerful Morning Routine!

When Nothing Else Works
How To Cure Your Lower Back Pain Fast!

Free Gift

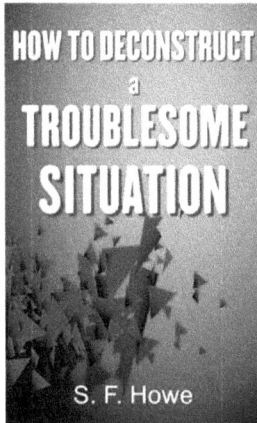

As our thanks to you for reading *The Bringer Discourses: On Waking Up to the Mind Control Programs of the Matrix Reality,* we would like you to download the bonus report, "How to Deconstruct a Troublesome Situation." Inside this report is a powerful technique that will help you strip any problem down to its core and give you the objectivity needed to find the best solution. To get your bonus gift, go to:

https://bit.ly/DeconstructSituation/

For those who seek higher dimensional perspectives in order to experience psychological and emotional freedom in the midst of everyday life.

Table of Contents

Author's Preface

The Waters of Knowledge

Welcome to *The Bringer Discourses: On Waking Up to the Mind Control Programs of the Matrix Reality*. You may be wondering who or what is The Bringer? As a spiritual psychologist and explorer of consciousness, I long ago discovered my ability to access higher dimensional knowledge. In so doing, The Bringer, a healer/awakener aspect of my consciousness, appeared as the conveyor of truth for this particular work.

The Bringer is here to take you on a journey into a virtual netherworld, for a behind-the-scenes glimpse of the realm you inhabit. This descent into darkness may seem to be a departure from my prime directive, which is to guide you on a path to peace, freedom and wholeness, but it is a necessary one. Though it is only a partial view of the total picture, as in peering through a keyhole, enough is revealed to accomplish my original intent for writing this book.

By recognizing the true nature of the realm you inhabit for the duration of your current story, you are encouraged to seek and cleave ever more closely to the truth of your being as One with Source.

As you read this book, remember that Consciousness is All and within Its infinite spaciousness this world is but a blip in time. Better to know what you are dealing with, in order to put things in context and thereby make the most of your lifetime.

In the words of The Bringer, *"With these writings, I bring you the waters of knowledge to help quench your thirst for psychological freedom."*

Introducing The Bringer

I am the Voice that speaks from the deepest, most hidden recesses of your being. I have been called many things, among them the 'still, small voice' or 'the way, the truth and the life.' You have been told by the wise in every language in the world to listen for me. Yet how many of you are able to hear my message?

Today I again bring truth to a fallen world, fallen not by your own deliberate design, but by the combination of intent from controlling factions and your subjugation to their malfeasance. From a higher perspective none of this has happened, but I speak to you where you are, struggling in the midst of your dream of reality, and I bring hope and healing if only you can hear my words.

There is the outer world and the inner world. Both are necessary for Divine Expression, and you, playing your part in the outer world, are necessary for Divine Expression as well. No matter how small you think yourself to be, how inadequate or unqualified, you are an inseparable part of the Whole, the One Being of God. As such, you are sourced from Divine Consciousness and have all that Consciousness bestows on its creation, meaning everything, for Consciousness is the substance of all form.

It is hard to comprehend how you are this struggling human living in an increasingly crowded and desolate world bereft of the love and light you yearn for with all your heart while at the same time holding the glorified status of Infinite Being in human expression. Yet it is so, and even more so is the truth of your eternal being and glory, the beauteous radiance of your countenance, visible only to those with eyes to see.

Introducing The Bringer

I am The Bringer, and I have come to open your hearts and minds so that you may birth a new world of love and peace. These words cannot fall on deaf ears even if you turn away, because you and I are one, and there can be no separation from the truth of your being. You have called me into your reality, dreamed me into existence, for The Bringer exists within each one of you.

The hope of The Bringer arrives with your birth into the degraded reality called Earth, yet the battle for your soul begins right there as well. Forces conspire to make of you a counterfeit of your true self, all of this accomplished while you are a helpless infant, in the name of love. But the love of people on Earth is like a jagged shard of broken glass as compared to the perfect, smooth, gleaming surface of real love.

In this world of diverse cultures there are countless languages, each one altering neuronal development in the brain bio-computer in its own unique way. This results in a jigsaw puzzle world where each culture produces people who express as fragments of the Whole. With no culture allowing Wholeness to express, each instead specializes in its own peculiar distortion of human cognition such that the true human cannot be found and is not even known in your world. That is the sad truth about your planet.

With billions of incomplete humans sharing a small planet, each one a twisted fragment of their real self, only conflict, war and destruction can result. The real travesty, however, is how normal this seems to all of you, how habituated you are to the rabid insanity of your circumstances.

The good news is that I have come to open your eyes to the truth, to awaken you to your actual condition within the All and to expand your awareness of love, peace and oneness. I come with the glad tidings that you too are The Bringer, as you and I are one.

Every human birthed into this world is The Bringer, but none are aware of who they really are. Let us begin to shed light upon the darkness of mystification that has obfuscated your passage in this life.

Introducing The Bringer

In the following chapter we will consider the raw facts of your human existence in a virtual world which you believe to be real, the whys and wherefores, the roots of this strange deception and the opportunity it presents for all of you.

Chapter 1

Origins of Deception

You believe you grew in your mother's womb and were delivered into a physical world. Your science has all the data to support the solid, hard reality of this world, including how it evolved to its current state from bacteria eons ago. Science, however, continues to evolve, though always behind the truth by quite a few steps; but the scientific vanguard touches upon it, trying to discern the truth of existence in this universe.

It would not serve the controllers of your reality to have science discover and reveal the truth, for it would destabilize the planetary population and put their agendas in jeopardy. Nothing occurs on this planet that does not serve the overlords.

That said, science is a shill of the controllers and even when authentic researchers make brilliant discoveries, their knowledge is marginalized and/or takes so long to reach the masses in a comprehensible format that old beliefs persist and earlier programming perpetuates ad infinitum.

If the cutting edge of science were to be believed, you would know yourself to live in a holographic reality, a veritable virtual world, your seemingly solid, physical presence no more substantial than an avatar in a video game. Notice how that conflicts with your subjective experience of being in a three-dimensional physical world governed by time.

In fact, your world is fashioned from the Infinite Field of Consciousness with its own limiting coordinates. The purpose of a world such as yours is to explore diversity in all of its amazing variety and allow Higher Consciousness to add to its storehouse of data through the manifold experiences of countless human expressions.

That said, the planet you inhabit has undergone its own transformation from a potential paradise of freedom and diversity to a madhouse of poverty, disease, overcrowding, crime, war and destruction. The real surprise is in how few of you grasp the conditions in the bigger picture much less question why they exist.

It is hard to lift one's eyes above the immediate four walls you inhabit, the needs of the loved ones in your home, looking after yourself, the work in front of you, the errands to be run, the friends and family to be kept up with, not to mention the endless repairs, problems and other issues you are tasked with unto your last breath on Earth.

Yes, it is true, your last moment on Earth is perhaps your only utterly and truly peaceful moment. That is when you finally know there are no more problems to be solved, people to be pacified and things to do. That last breath, if you are still conscious, brings with it extraordinary relief, for only then do you dare allow yourself to feel how burdensome the stretch of years called 'your life' really were.

Many of you believe your consciousness ends there. Others hold expectations of paradise or reincarnation, and everything in between. The Bringer exists outside of the time and space coordinates of your temporal reality, planet Earth, and assures you that your awareness can never die because you arise from within the Infinite Consciousness of the All. However, what does await is a reckoning of sorts, where you integrate your experience and decide on the next experience desired for your consciousness. For you are a spark of the Whole, where each spark is the Whole in individualized expression, thus allowing It to have a more complete discovery of Its own infinite potential.

The Whole exists eternally, infinitely and ever-presently. It can never not be there. And you, as a spark of the Whole exist within it forever and ever. Therefore, even while you appear to live in this heavy existence under the illusion of physical, you, in fact, labor in a virtual, non-physical world created by Mind which has manipulated the Field of Consciousness to create your unique reality.

The only way out is the way through. You cannot escape your condition within this 'board game,' but you can awaken while within 'the game,' and in knowing the truth about your condition as well as all of its fascinating ramifications, you shall be set free to embrace the forbidden truth of your world.

You are God. Yes, that is the truth. You are the Consciousness, the One, the All, the Everything that is Omniscient, Omnipresent, and Omni-Directional. How can that be, you ask? I am nothing, just a struggling, suffering human, subject to the weather, to the food supply, to the elements, to the other people, to employment or the lack thereof, to the needs of my children, to my health, etc. etc.

Humans are the illusion of 'human.' The meaning of the word itself is God-man, and that is what you are, an individualized representation of God in human form within a virtual world, possessing all that God is, meaning possessing the ability to access the consciousness of God and express the brilliance, uniqueness and goodness of the Whole embodied as You.

But you do not express as God, The Bringer, until you realize that you are The Bringer; that your I Am is the I Am of Source Consciousness. It is in the realization of this truth and of that state of consciousness that you bring into existence your Whole expression as God-man. Until this lifting of your own consciousness occurs through your own intent, nothing can bring you that realization.

Awakening to truth is not a dispensation from a higher self, not a discovery made after fasting and long spiritual practice, not the result of a transmission by an 'enlightened' guru. It is simply the raising of your own awareness to the highest state possible and your active realization of the true condition of your Being, meaning that part of you which is aware of Being the I Am. Once this realization has been accessed, it must be cultivated through repeated reaching for that state, it must be romanced, it must be danced. There is nothing outside of your human awareness in this life that will help you know God except for this movement in your own consciousness which you make willingly and deliberately when you orient toward your Godself.

In the following chapters, be prepared to discover the myriad ways in which your culture, no matter where in the world you may be, has worked to limit you, distract you and hide from you the truth of your real power. This begins and ends with the core beliefs instilled through cultural programming about your true identity and the nature of reality, and also includes a vast network of subconscious beliefs about 'the right way to live' promulgated by your institutions, not least of which is the family. These programs will be exposed one by one until you have a full view of the mental prison you have been encased in your entire life.

Chapter 2

The Family Program

At the core of social mind control is The Family Program, for if you control the family you control the world. The institutions, such as religion, education, health care, media and government, function as the disseminators of the conditioning that The Family translates for its own use and installs in its young.

Running directly beneath The Family Program is The Good Life Program, which sets the stage for all the false beliefs that must be absorbed by new arrivals into the culture, meaning the newborns. Closely aligned with The Good Life Program is The Scarcity Program, ensuring that the search for the good life is never-ending by keeping it visible but just out of reach. One could not exist without the other, and they both will be discussed at length in later chapters.

The Family Program requires a woman to give birth or otherwise acquire a child to be identified as 'her own.' A male partner or husband is usually part of the equation, playing the role of provider and back-up assistant to the primary caretaker, the mother. Modern day attempts to have the male fulfill the role of the female in order to achieve the illusion of equal parenting, which is a sub-belief of the Family Program, often fall short as nature did not design men to be primary caretakers of infants, although a father may make much effort and insistence upon rising to the occasion.

The mother, who typically greets the arrival of a child with intense ambivalence, may secretly be grateful to be free to go back to work while also carrying the enhanced status of being a mother. If she stays home, she may find it harder to deny the sacrifice that is being asked of her: to pretend that having a child makes her whole and thereby agree to remain permanently incomplete, to forget who she really is and never unearth the gifts that remain latent within her Infinite Being, to live vicariously through another's life and find self-esteem in the other's very existence, in their accomplishments and in the social approval of being a mother.

On the other hand, the cultural programming ensures a disconnect with the true self that will render most men and women so lacking in ability and higher purpose that they will automatically conform to the socially-approved position of making it all about The Family. Thus, the inevitable march of virtually the entire population. And where are they marching to? The Family Program ensures that they are marching toward the formation of their own families as inexorably as soldiers, since time immemorial, have marched in formation to war.

No cow is more sacred than the sacred cow of Motherhood. A woman looks at her child as a perfect extension of herself and proceeds to mold it with all the programming she possesses within her. This is how the world is made, one heavily programmed and deeply asleep parent imprinting heavy programming and deep sleep on a vulnerable, unconditioned child, all of this done in service of 'giving my child a better life.' The relationship between the parents works well when they are fully agreed on the exact conditioning to provide, as there are sidebars and variations in the programs that allow conflicted parents to engage in incessant argument and debate. But the end result is assured. All the quirks and peculiarities of that culture will be duplicated by the child as if they were stamped out on an assembly line.

In this way, the idiosyncrasies of that culture are passed on from generation to generation, creating a population skewed toward a specific, limited way of being. Thus you have enforced cultural duality in the obvious strengths arising within the culture's area of specialization along with obvious glaring weaknesses where the culture falls short.

The resulting child is raised in The Family to be exactly as the perfect little girl and little boy of that culture should be and has the complete package of beliefs and limitations and quirks and peculiarities that each gender is designed to have.

The Family derives its programs from the dominant beliefs of the institutions and locales that have most involvement with the child. These usually include the schools, the medical staff, the church and the community agencies, as well as the extended family, friends of the family and any other adults, such as sports coaches, tutors, music or dance teachers, babysitters, etc., who come into regular contact with the child.

To oppose the dominant beliefs and practices of the local culture is to expose the child to ridicule, bullying and rejection. Therefore, The Family is highly motivated to help their child fit in. Thus, in the name of preparing their child for a good life, The Family caves to the demands of their culture more often than not, even where parents have themselves awakened to a higher truth and do not necessarily agree. The cultural pressure to fit in is intense and perpetual, thereby determining the fate of the child. The parents know their child must be made to fit the

Procrustean bed of acceptable society or be a pariah while but a fledgling in the world.

Shaping the child into the desired mold is never as easy as a parent would wish it to be, as children have within their hearts the buried voice of their true self trying to break them free. But whether it requires a beating, medication or other punishment, the parents persist in trying to control their child's behavior, convinced that the child will not make it in the world unless they conform to certain expectations. Invariably, the child rebels in its own way, creating a chasm with the parent. The love that is potential between a parent and child becomes marked by discord; the spirit of the child deeply wounded and scarred by a repeated lack of acceptance and allowance.

This wounded child is also dependent on their parent's love and eventually finds a way to accede to the demands of the parent even though it must sacrifice its deepest truth. Rebellion alternates with surrender, demonstrating the gradual yet complete overtaking of the child by the prime directives of its culture. Eventually, the natural tendency to object to being rethreaded by cultural warps becomes suppressed and the child fully acquiesces to the culture and to the family expectations.

Each culture demands a horrifying tribute from its natives – the relinquishing of your true self and your connection to the Unlimited Consciousness of Infinite Being in exchange for the opportunity to peer out at the world through a narrow slit fashioned by language and false beliefs and call it reality.

Yet when all is said and done, the young adult feels completely unique and is unaware of the soul-destroying compromise that delivered them to their actual circumstance as a cookie-cutter replication of their culture, though a few may possess gifts that survived the assault on their true being.

The Family Program guarantees that the parents and the children shall adhere to the demands of their culture and perpetuate its traditions and beliefs. Invariably, this precludes knowing the truth of your being as Infinite Consciousness or becoming awake to the gifts that Infinite Being bestows.

In the next chapter we will take a look at The Good Life Program which underlies The Family Program and is the bulwark of the cynical lies perpetuated by all cultural institutions.

Chapter 3

The Good Life Program

A core requirement of The Good Life Program is your total submission to the demands of the system and the institutions that run it, while consciously believing you are pursuing your dreams. Each element of The Good Life Program, traced back to its roots, reveals a false belief accepted as truth. There can be no truth in The Good Life Program because it begins and ends with the denial of who you really are. It is designed to entrap you, instill a sense of dependency and helplessness, and bombard you with limitational social programming. This chapter aims to explore how this is accomplished and what it means for you.

It begins with a dream, a compelling urge to have a certain kind of life. If you are a female, it may include childhood fantasies of achieving fame as an actress or ballerina, floating down the aisle to become somebody's wife, living in a beautiful home with designer furnishings and decor, and raising adorable children. All this while you dress perfectly for every occasion and maintain the slender, youthful appearance of a model.

For boys, it may begin with childhood dreams of being number one at sports or another talent, admired by others and in demand, rich and powerful in the world, able to get any girl they desire, and eventually evolves into dreams of a successful career, wealth, a beautiful, faithful wife and adoring children.

Where do these fantasies come from? Most people assume it is normal to want success, a mate, a home, children and all good things. In fact, children see their parents seeking their own version of the good life and imagine the same or better for themselves. One might say that the fantasy comes from observing their parents, from reading books and magazines, from what they learn in school, watch on television or see in the movies. But what is the true source of The Good Life Program, and how does it get installed in every child?

The Good Life Program begins with a child's acceptance of their world as it appears to be. It begins with learning about **the paths open to members of thei**r culture **and thei**r gender, **and picturing them**self in one of those paths. Some paths seem readily available through the education system, others through developing certain gifts or talents. A child dreams without hindrance, imagines being their greatest self. The child seeks its extreme good, including glorious love, work, and personal fulfillment. Nothing can stop a child from believing in their dream and allowing it to drive their actions in everyday life. Only when financial limitations of the parent or gender role violations arise and slap the child in the face, do they face reality. At this stage, their personal limitations are not a factor, but the external world certainly is. The child imagines a workaround, and in their fantasy life, everything is possible.

The irony is that even when supposedly facing reality, The Good Life Program offers one red herring after another. This is your route to happiness, no, that is, no try this, or this, maybe you will find your happiness here rather than there. In this way, young people pursue different avenues of happiness, but they all lead to the same place and are just different spokes of the one wheel. Once grown, the child realizes the limitations in their dream, whether those limitations are simply the difficulty of making it happen at all or the flatness of the reality of living that dream. What happened to the rich, lush dreamscape that drove all that followed, leading to this moment?

Unfortunately, the rich, lush landscape was constructed of programming that allowed the child to believe it was pursuing its happiness only to reach the dead end of the real experience. Why is the real experience a dead end? For those who don't question, it is perceived as an arrival. But the idealism attributed to the arrival cannot survive the onslaught of reality. What is this reality? Nothing in the system is designed to bring joy and fulfillment. The system is a necessary evil to sustain the ones who benefit by it. The child dreaming with excitement about their future, so eager to be a grown up and take their place in the world, quickly learns that the dream of a good life serves its own purpose and cares nothing for their needs. From the start, the child is bent in one direction only, the direction that serves the system, no matter that it distorts their entire being to do so.

That realization comes far too late. There is a family to support, children to look after, a struggling mate suppressing their own vast disillusionment. Yet all soldier on with a pretense of good cheer, secretly baffled, offering the same falsehoods to their children that brought them to this unholy place, rationalizing their choices and seeking the silver lining, even believing that God directed their path to this very moment. And in so doing, they feel moved to express gratitude for this Good Life that they are living, a life that is the embodiment of what they were supposed to do, what they still sincerely believe they wanted to do from the start.

If a child did not admire the glitzy idols of their era, such as the movie stars, the sports stars, the ones in the limelight who present as living, human extremes with everything everyone wants, they might quietly find within themselves something to admire, a burgeoning talent perhaps, a skill of some kind, a way of being in the world. If a child knew that they were cut from the cloth of the Infinite, their own self would be viewed as endlessly worthy and endlessly gifted. How exciting to plumb the depths of one's own vast being, to explore one's own potential, and aim to strike oil within those depths; each child on a hero's journey to find the secret elixir within themself and bring it back so that the world may gain from their discoveries.

This is a far different story than The Good Life Program which constricts the child, feeds them full of fantasies based on external imagos and consigns them to adapting to standards set by others next to whom they feel lesser and unworthy. While they struggle to fit in, to find their place in the world, they finally submit and move forward into one of the acceptable paths, further weighed down by the inevitable wife, husband and parent roles automatically restricting their lives within specific parameters that dictate much of what they do thereafter.

Once the children are born, the parents no longer feel the significance of their own being, except in its relationship to the child as mother and father. The child comes first; the parent subjugates themselves to the needs of the child and to the manifold aspects of raising a young person within their culture. What was once potentially a glorious endeavor to unveil the diamond hidden within their own being is now a vicarious endeavor of helping a child become all that it can be within the limits of its culture. In this way, each parent dies to their own potential in service of preparing another human being for use in the system, who in turn will die to their own potential when they bear their own children in the society.

The Good Life Program revolves around breeding and raising children. It encourages an animal level existence that is in denial of the higher consciousness living within all beings. Rather than allowing each being to find its own true place in the order of things, to find the ways in which they shine and to develop that to greatness, allowing everyone to bring their brilliant light to bear on their culture, making of their culture a radiant tapestry, the individual's light is reduced to its dimmest ebb. Financial, social and emotional burdens replace the possibility of full human expression free of outdated concepts of what life in the Earth realm is meant to be.

At the bedrock of both The Family Program and Good Life Program lies The Scarcity Program which drives all of the false belief systems dominating the cultures of planet Earth. In the next chapter, we shall explore The Scarcity Program and its insidious effects.

Chapter 4

The Scarcity Program

Whenever you have a thought telling you that you are less than, or that you cannot have something or be something, you are running the Scarcity Program, one of the most powerful and ubiquitous of all forms of mind control in your realm. This program alone maintains all the others and is the glue that keeps the entire limitational mindset in place, thereby determining the fate of an entire world population.

And what is that fate? To remain enslaved to a system that cynically encodes you with false beliefs in order to keep you small and separate from your true potential even when you believe you are pursuing your fondest dreams!

Your existence is a dream within a dream. The first dream is that you are a biological entity born to 'live' on a planet that is perpetually orbiting in outer space until you, eventually, 'die.' The second dream, also known as the sub-creation, contains all the details of human limitational programming. Every negative thought and every appearance of loss, lack, deprivation or struggle has its roots in the second dream. These roots are so profoundly networked into human consciousness that awareness of your true being as the I Am of Creation is obliterated.

The identical twins, Scarcity and Limitation, run most people's lives from start to finish. Even many of the awakened ones believe that scarcity and limitation are intrinsic to this world. The belief in duality, up and down, light and dark, rich and poor, good and evil, fuels the perpetuation of extremes in your world. Duality is justified by the Genesis story in your bible, where the members of paradise, Adam and Eve, receive God's injunction to avoid eating the fruit of the Tree of Good and Evil. In violating His commands, awareness of opposites possess the early denizens of Eden, and duality is born.

Interestingly, even in the bible, the story begins and ends with activities of consciousness. Before eating the apple, there is oneness with God, which means surrender to Spirit; no awareness of opposites and no judgment of 'what is.' Once the knowledge of duality enters consciousness, Adam and Eve are cast out of Eden, having usurped God's place. Now they are living by human rules, condemned to survive by the sweat of their brow and to give birth in pain.

Duality is a core program of the realm you inhabit. Resolving duality is an activity that quietly occurs within your consciousness and restores you to God's grace. This is a key to escaping the pernicious effects of limitational programming that possess every one of you in every culture of your world throughout every nook and cranny of your planet. By turning this key you unlock the door to Oneness. In Divine Oneness, you surrender your position as director of your destiny and allow the Creator Source, that which is the true I Am of you, to direct all that you do.

Taking this step violates every rule of scarcity programming, that desperate struggle to survive which surfaced the moment you were banished from Eden. Now you vie for scraps, giving it important names: jobs, mates, children, possessions, social status, power, and exult in your dubious victories. Locked from birth to death in a silent war to assert your superiority, you cannot, nay dare not, give up your attempts to control reality to a faceless, nameless God! Yet this is exactly what is required for you to free yourself from the torments of scarcity programming. You must return to Eden where the price of admission, and the means of restoring your true being as One with God, is to let go of control moment by moment and seek guidance from within.

We speak here of relinquishing the ego, otherwise known as the false self, and allowing the higher part of you, your I Am consciousness, which lurks in the shadows like an understudy awaiting the director's nod, to take its place as the I of you.

One returns to Eden by taking the journey back to Source; in so doing, you discover the life you were meant to live. Scarcity programming imposes the sub-creation, the limitational existence you have led until now which catered to the cultural quirks and desires of an altered self divorced from contact with True Being. You will continue to live in this way until you die unless you wrap up your gear and head Home.

Very few will attempt this arduous journey due to their indoctrination by The Religion Program, thus ensuring a sleeping populace ripe for the picking. Read on to learn how, like all programs, The Religion Program was installed to serve the control system while it appears to benefit and soothe the people.

Chapter 5

The Religion Program

Every human being hungers for truth and has at one time or another pondered the true nature of their existence. This natural tendency for expansion of thought could bring realizations of truth if not for The Religion Program. Nothing has been more effective in limiting and controlling consciousness than the imprisonment of minds by organized religion, and, specifically, by the religion of your birth. Through this conditioning, an individual's worldview and spiritual perspective are distorted before they are even old enough to try to form an original thought.

Most follow the dictates of their religion, whether consciously or unconsciously. But while religion, like all programs, contains at its core a kernel of spiritual truth, the true purpose of religion has always been the same across the world: mind control. Keep the struggling masses nose to grindstone, content to serve their masters by appeasing and comforting them with false, rigidly enforced, religious beliefs.

These beliefs are founded in lies and fantasies about the supernatural. They arise from the supposition that the human being is hardly better than a wild animal, inherently evil and immoral, and seeks only its own selfish good, thereby requiring management through strict external rules and motivation by fear. However, if you are 'good' and follow the dictates of your religion, you can variously expect to be reborn into a better life, avoid going to hell, be resurrected by the Messiah or enjoy pleasures in heaven which you denied yourself on earth.

In the great con game known as religion, most religious fantasies are fueled by cornerstone stories of great men sent by God who perform miracles and become the focus of your worship.

These tales, accepted by vast numbers of people as naively as a child awaits Santa Claus' delivery of presents on Christmas Eve, form the bulwark of The Religion Program. Though nothing will limit you more than worshipping another human being while also believing that God is a powerful man in the sky who sends down other men as His representative, such worship is in fact the basis for most world religions.

Religion asks that you deny your true reality as a spark of the Divine. It requires your denial of your spiritual Source and its ever present reality as the very Ground of Being within which you arise. This is an enormous leap for a human being who knows on some level the truth of their being. You are asked to live as if you are a biological creature, in fact, just another form of animal life with perhaps a bit more intelligence, though even that little bit of intelligence has been cynically and deliberately reduced by the religious establishment through the inculcation of religious lies and fantasies, peaking in the belief in idols.

The essence of your planetary reality is paradox, and there is no lack of it in your acceptance of the concept of a messiah, whether one that has long ago arrived or one who will arrive someday. The paradox lies in denying your own inseparable connection to the godhead in favor of believing that a separate God once sent supernatural representatives whose current mouthpieces are the clerics.

The moment you pray to another being or are controlled by a human, whether an anthropomorphic version of God, another physical person or an imaginary historical entity, you have stepped away from truth and are lost to the programming. Yet this is considered not only natural and normal, but the only correct human behavior in most cultures across the world to this day.

A higher dimensional perspective reveals that those who accept religion are harnessed to a low to mid-range bandwidth of consciousness that resonates to their specific belief system. Therefore, the process of consciously moving away from those beliefs is unlikely except for those who inhabit the highest range of that bandwidth and, as such, have the innate potential for a move into more advanced territories of consciousness.

The move away from religion is the first step of an individual in the early stages of awakening. Though often met with persistent, disturbing cries from those who cannot bear to lose you to truth, which they are programmed to view as lies, nothing can stop a persona who is called to truth.

What begins as a turning away from the empty religious rituals and tall tales espoused by clerics and their 'sacred documents' continues as a search for answers. Sometimes this means the persona goes from one religion to another, not yet grasping the false basis and true purpose of all religions. And what is that purpose, you might ask?

Nothing has served the controllers more in maintaining control of an individual's everyday behavior than his adherence to religion. The acceptance of a religion, particularly the concept that you are born into a religion and are therefore permanently identifiable as that religion, auto-matically brings with it the programming of guilt.

Between the socially enforced induction into the religion of your birth, along with all of its limiting beliefs, and the unconscious guilt and social rejection that accompanies denial or aban-donment of that religion when an individual seeks freedom of thought, the persona is set up for perfect management by religious figures and religious dictates.

Awaiting the rare, awakening individual who cannot find truth in their religion of birth or in other organized religions, is the compromised spiritual marketplace which contains all manner of new age teachings. These teachings may be considered the golden handcuffs of religion. They appear to encourage human potential, diversity and self-actualization while ensnaring the indi-vidual in another set of limiting beliefs mixed with some higher truth.

Those who manage the masses fear above all their awakening to truth about their own higher consciousness and Oneness with I Am. Denial of this truth requires concerted and persistent effort as every human being is immersed in and sourced from the very Consciousness they are being asked to pretend does not exist. This is an uphill battle for the controllers who have made it their mission to understand all the quirks of human psychology and behavior so that they can better control the people. Add to that a built-in array of energetic technologies and other toxic forces deployed from behind the scenes, which beset the individual, convincing them of their smallness and dependence on the establishment for survival, and you have a huge populace reduced to the bare minimum level of consciousness for easy and successful management by the few in power.

Additionally, spirituality and religion are often confused as the same thing in the conventional worldview, though nothing could be further from the truth. As a result, people who spurn religion may be written off as atheistic when in fact their spirituality may be their strongest and most profound quality. Spirituality presupposes an interest in the true nature of reality. That journey to knowledge requires relinquishing all the toys of childhood, most especially religion, its fairy tales and its false sense of security.

Imagine a world free of control of the masses by religionists and prophets. Individuals would find in their inner self the strength to be more than they ever imagined they could be. On the other hand, you might imagine that those of the lowest vibrational sectors would rampage without the tempering factor of religious beliefs and the priests that enforce them. It could also be said that when a population has been programmed from birth to total distortion of truth, the 'natural' individual may be incapable of regulating their own behavior free of external controls, and would become a danger to society, thereby appearing to justify the ongoing control tactics of religion.

There have always been those who care little for the well-being of others and, given half a chance, would take what they want with impunity. Fear grips the subconscious of the world, knowing that those of a finer make are vulnerable to the primitive urges of an unmanaged lower sector. Add to that the pleasures, advantages and accomplishments of those in higher vibrational stories denied to the aggrieved, jealous, lower consciousness individuals who thrive on blaming others, and it further implies that a move away from religion could in fact raise a threat.

In actuality, the process of consciously moving away from religion or other false spiritual programming is limited to those whose story permits such expansion of consciousness. That understanding completely removes concern over the unwashed masses running amok with their new sense of freedom if religion were somehow removed from the equation. In fact, other false belief systems have already been installed to maintain the necessary order as needed and have been designed to fulfill the same function that religion currently does. As of this writing, an agenda has long been in the works to gradually weaken the grip of religion while shifting the people to another locus of control.

The controllers play the long game, which by necessity contains numerous overlapping agendas, some of which stretch across centuries, and others which run for shorter lengths, much of it experimental, none of it perfect, yet all designed to ultimately move an entire world populace towards isolation and consolidation for easier control.

In the next chapter we will explore one of the most powerful methods of self-limitation ever devised. By this we refer to The Health Program. In understanding how health is used against you to keep you dependent on the very system you need to be free of for optimal health, we add another piece to the puzzle of how you are re-duced to a manageable biological entity and experimented on at will, not unlike bacteria in a petri dish, rather than respected as a creator god in your own right.

Chapter 6

The Health Program

Though you have often heard it said that the body has the ability to heal itself, have you ever wondered why your body seems to need the ongoing ministrations of the medical establishment? Enter The Health Program, which ensures disease and the dependence on medical healers, who in turn dispense the drugs they have been taught to prescribe. Not only is the body led as far away from its own source of healing by the programmed medical professionals and their elixirs, but the truth about the body and its ills, were it revealed, would never be believed.

In a pseudo-physical realm beset in all directions by hard and solid illusions of physicality, the illusion of having a physical body is the most difficult belief to transcend. But by allowing that deeply ingrained belief to be put aside for the time being and pretending to accept the unreality of the body, we can see clearly the depth of the false programming and lies in The Health Program, as a body that does not really exist cannot become ill and does not need to be healed by either the self or the medical establishment. That which is not real, but only appears to be real, can never develop a real illness but only an illusion of illness.

The understanding of the body as symbolic and not literal is to know the true nature of body. And what does it symbolize? It symbolizes you, your presence in the story. Viewed in its raw, unvarnished truth, the rest of your illusion world must also be understood for what it is – nothing more than a dream world, a stage for a play with you as the lead. Yes, it feels intensely real in the living of it, just as your night dreams can feel completely real, but it is no more substantial than the dreams of night which fade in the light of day.

For detailed information about the nature of the physical illusion world, please read the foundational work by S. F. Howe, *Matrix Man: How to Become Enlightened, Happy and Free in an Illusion World.*

The human drama is so realistic that the idea of it being virtual and ephemeral may be hard to digest. Yet that is exactly how it was designed to be. If it were any less real, you would not be fully absorbed in your story, and the purpose of your story could not be fulfilled. The story that rises above the mundane must be fraught with shadows and light, multi-layers of conflict, ambivalence, ambiguity and heartbreak as well as moments of ineffable joy and supernal bliss. In other words, it demands a rip-roaring adventure into the physical transmogrification of your heart and soul. You walk within your Self, your path containing exquisite meaning for the Great One that designed your consciousness and materialized you in the story.

The conventional perspective would have you believe that your consciousness arises from the brain within the head portion of your physical body, that this body is solid, three-dimensional and utterly vulnerable. It is no wonder the over-whelming majority are owned lock, stock and barrel by The Health Program. In believing the foundational lie that you are a physical body in a physical world, you guarantee ownership by the only things that can save you – doctors, medical procedures and pharmaceuticals. This one lie succeeds in stripping you of power and majesty, and ensures your slavery to medical cures. At the highest level, all medical cures are no-thing and have no ability to hurt you or help you; but the beliefs about the medicines form The Health Program, and those beliefs bring results in your body according to your belief.

You may be wondering how a medicine can harm you with its side effects, as it sometimes does, if you have been programmed to believe it will heal you. This question highlights a most interesting aspect of this world of duality in that what may heal also has the power to harm under certain conditions, and all according to your beliefs.

The Health Program

Your programming around your body and wellness is not only occurring consciously through what you see, read or hear, but it is also occurring unconsciously through the collective unconscious. Beliefs within the collective are as powerful, or more powerful, than conscious information in determining, for example, a drug's side effect, even when you may have never consciously heard of the drug. In this way, you are continually programmed consciously and unconsciously, whether awake or asleep.

Because nothing is real and it is all a dream, your programming and its effects are designed to serve your story. While this may be the case, it still does not mean that the body was actually ill or that the medicine or treatment healed something when nothing was really there.

Whether it is your belief empowering the treatment to rid you of the disease, or the medical establishment's belief in the drug's effectiveness along with their belief in its dangerous side effects, such health dramas occur within a dream reality enacted with all the tiniest details in place to convince you of their veracity.

Once you accept that the body does not create and thereby cannot develop an ailment, the idea of healing via self or another loses its charm. Healing is seen for what it is – an invention of the medical establishment or the medical establishment's mirror – alternative medicine. Any treatment presupposes the belief that the ailment is real and that the cure is real and can fix what never existed in the first place.

Many, if not all, human programs are designed to change, fix or improve something that does not exist in the first place. This is never more apparent than in the issues of gender identity conflict and gender dysphoria which have surfaced on the world scene with a vengeance and which are addressed at length in S. F. Howe's book, *Transgender America: Spirit, Identity and the Emergence of the Third Gender.* If you are interested in discovering how your true identity as an Infinite Being has been exchanged for a physical illusion-based gender identity, along with all the bugaboo issues and conflicts arising from that single false construct of gender identity, please read *Transgender America*.

A close cousin of The Health Program is The Science Program, which we explore in the very next chapter. With science raised up as the new religion, there can be no rest for the weary seeking truth.

Science is the golden calf of modern life; it seeks to replace an individual's direct knowing of the true nature of reality with a dependence on questionable interpretations of ever-changing 'scientific facts' and hypotheses. Like a snake eating its own tail, you are repeatedly brought full circle into the ever-deepening lies about the true nature of the reality that scientific research purports to explain.

Chapter 7

The Science Program

As part of the denial of your true being as the Ultimate, you are given a new religion that pretends to serve up all the answers. That religion is Science. With research elevated to the level of idol worship, and scientific studies and findings shorn of all spiritual possibility constituting its 'bible,' science proposes questionable and ever-evolving theories that are only relevant to the era in which the theories spring and the agenda the theories serve.

Scientific facts are theories that have been accepted as fact, first in the minds of scientists, and then filtered down to the people. These theories turned into facts are derived from the results of scientific research that have been designed and interpreted subjectively, and from extremely limited perspectives, the only way scientific research can be interpreted.

Theories, however, are not the same thing as truth, and the non-physical truth of physical reality can never be proven by the theories of science. Even quantum physics, science's last outpost of creative thought, has not made the case for the truth it ultimately purports to prove, that the world is a manifestation of Consciousness, safely renamed The Information Field. If it did, this would already be integrated into the worldview of the everyday person and have drastically altered religious beliefs. Instead, quantum physics' theories, in all their awkward and at times fanciful varieties, while closer to truth, are relegated to theoretical not factual. Therefore, ever-changing scientific 'facts' based on a false origin theory – the belief in the reality of a physical world formed through evolution after a 'big bang' – firmly remains 'god.'

Scientific theories can never be truth and the non-physical truth of reality can never be proven by the theories of science. The two are divorced from one another by their very nature – apples and oranges – and never the twain shall meet. Yet Science is upheld as the ultimate source of knowledge about the true nature of reality.

Holding up lies as truth is a normal part of the mind control programming in your reality where everything is reversed. The purpose of reversal is to confuse and divert the vulnerable human mind from its own inner self where truth resides about all things. Science teaches you to distrust your self, the source of truth, and to accept a backwards, upside down, inside out version of reality. It begins with lies about evolution, lies about the greater reality in which your realm resides, lies about your own physical body and lies about who and what you are, where you came from and what your true purpose is.

Science would have you believe you evolved from fish in the sea that eventually made land over billions of years. It further describes prehistoric monsters, known as dinosaurs, and primitive man. It brandishes artifacts such as fossils, bones, ancient tools and cave paintings, along with the analysis of carbon layers, to support a false science. This science is taught in every school in the western world and viewed as irrefutable fact. Yet nothing could be further from the truth.

What would happen if people were taught the truth: that they exist in a non-physical reality and temporarily arise within it, as does the illusion world or place in which they find themselves? All of existence can be reduced to the simple Awareness of Being in a body in a place. The story told to the human population is a fairy tale, meant to encourage ignorance, dependency, emotional immaturity and mental weakness. This is the sad and persistent fate for human beings born into your world.

By design, these lies and suppressive beliefs are posited, 'proven,' and spewed out into the public arena as fact by scientists and their adherents. For when a being is systematically deprived of truth, he cannot access his power and be his natural self. He expresses a fraction of his abilities and becomes a veritable shadow of his true self.

The Science Program

Even when science appears to meld with spirit as in quantum reality theories, the truth is distorted and the primal spiritual nature of existence sidestepped by scientific babble and its related antics such as string theory, the singularity, alternate realities and quantum physics exercises. Even those exercises prove that the moment consciousness is applied to anything, that thing changes, i.e., perception changes a viewed reality.

With this kind of confusion, science can happily theorize about multiverses, big bangs, parallel dimensions and probable realities, but make it all sound like scientific fantasy. Science does love its fantasy and is happy to speculate with its imbalanced left-brain thinking that makes of spiritual reality a Star Trek-like TV show. In other words, scientific truth is anything but the truth, which can be known directly by every human being who allows themself to think for themself.

Thinking for yourself begins with questioning and ultimately ignoring everything science has found to be true. All phenomena depend on interpretation, which depends on perspective, which is subject to change when a phenomenon is viewed. There can be no truth founded in science, none whatsoever. Truth cannot be proven, is not scientific and is not quantifiable or able to be known through logic. It is direct knowing of the true nature of reality.

Direct knowing is the enemy of science in your world and given little respect or credence. If it is not supported by scientific research, it cannot be true. Yet that is exactly the situation; truth can only be known directly; it can never be proven in the scientific sense.

For the average, heavily programmed person, this is a conundrum solved only by being ignored. After all, science has all the answers, and where answers are lacking, science promises to be working on a new theory based on research.

The Science Program, while seeming to attract the most intelligent minds in your culture, actually takes highly programmed intellects and uses them as its mouthpiece. They are the true believers, and they serve the important function of guiding the thinking of your leaders, pundits and educators. Science co-opts the intelligence of the brightest, feeds them lies in the guise of accepted truth, and builds their cache in the world where they serve to transmit these lies to their colleagues and eventually to the masses. By owning the brightest and using them to disseminate lies as fact with great authority, the controllers ensure the perpetuation of The Science Program as it continues to develop and evolve for the trapping of programmed human minds into ever-deepening labyrinths of lies.

What is the reason for this ongoing distortion of truth in favor of lies? To an extent, it is self-sustaining because the great Science is actually the poor man's truth. Solid reality and other scientific constructs must be defended, supported and 'proven' so as to confirm all the false facts people have been taught from the beginning about the true nature of reality. As the control agenda evolves, which it inevitably does, and new ideas are introduced, they too become extensions of scientific theory supported by scientific research. In this way, science allows itself to perpetually contradict itself, which means it can never be truth. The most revered knowledge in your culture is in fact a ludicrous, backward and tortured interpretation of reality, subject to change at will, and with the purpose of directing attention away from or obfuscating the truth.

The introduction of these ideas begins in early life through The Education Program, which indoctrinates children and youth with a veritable encyclopedia of false beliefs presented as facts. This powerful arm of the programming monolith is explored in the following chapter.

Chapter 8

The Education Program

Acornerstone of all the other programs described in this book is The Education Program. While purporting to edify and elevate the population, preparing young people for a vital place in the world, education actually serves to dissociate all students from truth, lock them into their left brain, and feed them so-called facts about their reality that they must memorize and regurgitate in order to receive the approval of their teachers.

In The Education Program, educators serve as professional indoctrinators, although many have no knowledge of their real purpose and view their work as a sacred task to prepare the youth for their successful role in society.

Supported by the system with numerous holidays, long summer breaks, periodic paid sabbaticals, and an excellent pension at a relatively early retirement age, schoolteachers are seduced by their financial security and the various perks into following the system's educational program. They can be counted on to participate in all program changes even when they violate sanity and the sanctity of human freedom. This is how well the educators are used and bought to provide services of mind control and creativity reduction to the masses.

When children are delivered to higher educational locales where they will prepare for a specific profession or an executive level role in the culture, according to their interests and abilities, not least on the basis of funding provided by affluent parents, they will receive the finishing touches to their indoctrination and can be depended on to be 'set loose' as a professional or executive who will operate within the system.

All the others who lack the ability, interest or means to rise to a professional status find their place in the whole at whatever their level of functioning and carve their life out from there. Very little hope may be offered one who has not the means or the wherewithal to seek a higher level role in society, and thus they are condemned to a lesser quality of life.

The primary purpose of The Education Program is to prepare less educated workers for their basic roles as laborers, caretakers and tradesmen, and to brainwash those who are reaching for higher strata so that they do not engage in unprescribed services or teach unprescribed information to those entrusted in their care. One might say that basic education prepares a mind-controlled worker for a servant-level role in society and higher education prepares a livelier mind, and/or a mind supported by a livelier purse, for a managerial/professional role. For the latter, management here is primarily that of the ones who did not rise to a higher status and, to a lesser extent, of their peers who are suffering in their role.

We have little to say about the creatives of your culture as they are abandoned to their own devices, most failing to secure a foothold in society and forming a fringe layer where they have no real influence. It is not wise to seek a creative path in your culture unless you are content to provide the mediocre, emotionally immature, violent and sexually sadistic arts and media of the reigning pop culture. If so, you have successfully 'sold your soul,' and if at all gifted, may find support for your brand of creativity. Meanwhile, those who aspire to a higher purpose with their art soon find themselves doomed to present their work at small venues, or relegated to independent creative ventures short of capital, and ultimately fail to gain traction as they are meant to by the system.

The system does not support the free mind, the unopposed thought, the art of higher values and goodness. However, it does support, and will even bestow its most prestigious awards on, works of darkness, war, abuse, ugliness, the occult, violence, emotional dysfunction, emotional immaturity, sadistic sexuality and worse.

If reality were viewed with clarity by those who seek their place in society, they would not know which way to turn as every path leads into mental slavery. Because this realization is intolerable to a young mind seeking their place and dreaming of a fulfilled life, and because most minds have already been corrupted by lies posing as education, or by mind-numbing posing as learning, the truth of the future they prepare for, even the most glorious of dreams fulfilled, does not hold the slightest hope of being fulfilled when reality sets in and the young person recognizes the actual nature of their roles and purpose.

Of course, the most mind-controlled of the group never even question the programs put forth in this book, and they happily take on their role only to become increasingly disappointed with their lives without knowing why. The more awakened ones feel the disillusionment early and either quit for a lesser place in the world or soldier on despite their suffering. For those who are awake and suffer through it, their fate is to experience themselves as shills of the state, and this is what they must come to terms with as "my life," if they are honest with themselves.

From The Education Program, it is a short jump to The Success Program, which in turn is a subcategory of The Good Life Program. In the next chapter, we will view The Success Program without blinders, and you will see ever more clearly what the controllers of your education system have prepared for you.

Chapter 9

The Success Program

Whathat greater excitement than the dream of success arising within a young person's mind. They will "have it all," they will be rich, beautiful, happy, fulfilled, and lead a far more interesting life than their parents or siblings. When they look around they only see failure and smallness. Their parents radiate resignation and disappointment with their lives even while trying to convince their children that they are a happy family. They see their older, disillusioned siblings already lowering expectations. Everyone over the age of 25 looks worn out to them as they scan their immediate reality and try to make sense of their world. They must conclude: No one is happy but they will be! All they have to do is work hard, achieve their goals and then offer their well-honed gifts to the world, and the world will shower them with rewards and recognition.

The young person launches into their adolescence and early adulthood with a fire in the belly fueled by dreams of glory, of saving the world or some part of it, of being the one who makes a difference. Every happy, healthy youth wants to save the world and they believe themself to be on the plus side of the equation. On the minus side are all the youth who did not emerge from adolescence into a young adulthood of joy, excitement, hope and hubris, but are beset with emotional problems, financial problems, health issues, family issues, and the like. They have found early life a burden and can only hope their life will improve going forward. Some have a dream of escape – from their small town, from their family, from their job or school. The big city is the answer for many of these suffering souls, at least in their minds, offering hope of new opportunities and fresh energy. When they finally confront the financial limitations in their current life they realize their future dreams can never happen or must be relegated to someday. Someday they will be more, do more, have more. But most settle into a half-life of mindless work and future dreams sweetened by drugs and alcohol. If they do manage to leave, the big city presents its own challenges and is hardly the panacea they sought.

Whether happy, inspired youth or downbeat youth, life does not produce the expected joys even where success is conventionally achieved. While all things are relative and depend on perspective, the successful youth has made an accommodation to the expectations of his family and peers. This accommodation continues as he accepts conditions at work, in his new living environment and in his relationship or created family. There is nowhere for the successful youth to turn when he finally realizes that the reality of his life is burdened by tedious tasks, inopportune breakdowns, the expectations of others and, more profoundly, a lack of joy in carrying out his daily work. This may arrive as a mystery in the mind of the young worker who never expected this flat-ness of everyday life, barely lifted by small mo-ments of joy.

The sheer demands on his time bombarding him from the moment he wakes up to the moment he goes to sleep, makes of every day a feverish merry-go-round. That alone generates a chronic irritability which he keeps hidden because how can this irritability be expressed when he has it all and is so successful. It is a complete contradiction to everything he was programmed to expect from his new place in the world as a successful professional or executive. These feelings must be suppressed – the sense that there must be more – and, therefore, below the surface lurks a discomfort that will dog him all of his days, temporarily alleviated by alcohol and recreational drugs, burning off energy with friends, following his favorite media and sports, taking vacations and buying shiny new things. At the end of the day, emptiness has moved in and cannot be dislodged. But he will never question his choices, his decisions, his family, his culture, his education, and his world. That would be too confronting, too disloyal, too incendiary. These feelings are not even accessible except for brief moments when a true thought arises and he feels the vast emptiness of his life. This must be quickly driven back underground where it came from in order to preserve the sanctity of his life and, most especially, of his success.

For the youth of compromised dreams, he faces a sense of struggle that never lets up. Adding financial difficulties to the same burdens of young adulthood that beset the successful youth, the unhappy individual has long ago realized they will not save the world; they can barely take care of themself. The urge to be a change agent in society was long ago squelched, and the lesser youth exists from day to day, just trying to survive. Very little energy is given to higher thought about his reality as resignation has already set in. This is their life and how it will always be until, that is. the pipe dream held by all unhappy youth can be realized. While some pipe dreams occasionally come true and bring an improvement in circumstances, most of these attempts to achieve a modicum of success involve enormous effort, struggle and persistence. Few of those whose wills have already been compromised will have the strength to withstand the gap, the gale winds that muster against them, when they attempt to rise above their station. If they do manage to carve a place in the world and become one of the successful ones, they then need to confront the anguish attendant on success – that is, after the first flush. If they were burdened before, now they face even heavier responsibilities. The merry-go-round has just begun. They lifted themselves up by their bootstraps and now must hang by those bootstraps (until dead). At least, that is how it often feels to those who have clawed their way to some degree of success.

Abandoned by all who have made success their God is the realization of their oneness with their own divine true self. To attain that awareness takes time, takes privacy, takes attention to the inner life. In other words it requires a commit-ment that is often impossible for the average person living a conventionally successful life. The demands of the spouse, the children, the employer, the job, the house, the mortgage and the ongoing maintenance of all the above define most lives in your world, not to mention the pressures as well surrounding religious and family obligations, filling every waking moment of every day. This is the success they were programmed to have – the marvelous realization of a full life sourced in financial well-being.

Whether you are born to the success train, are one who hitched a ride and are hanging onto success by a thread, or one who can only dream, success is dangled in front of your nose from birth as the ultimate carrot. And why is success so important? Because it gives you the means to provide a higher quality of life for yourself and your family, garners the respect of your elders and peers, and presents more options for experiencing the fullness of life. But the higher you rise, the harder you fall. Therefore, of paramount importance is maintaining your place in the social order, maintaining your responsibilities, and continuing to receive the financial, ego and emotional kudos of your place in the world.

Where in the scheme of things is there room for knowing anything about the truth of your reality or for looking squarely at that empty hole in the center of your being and asking why it is there rather than justifying it away? It does not exist in the scheme of things, for that is how The Success Program entraps all of the youth before they have even begun to question the true nature of reality, if ever they will.

The Success Program is the most insidious of all the programs because it appears to offer so much and, therefore, deserves adherence. Rarely will an individual question the purpose of this program, the secret feeling of failure, of never being enough, that accompanies the lives of all who live within The Success Program, and the grip it continues to have on everyone because of the fear of failure – not just the failure they already know themselves to be – but public failure. As long as they appear to be successful, their cover is in place and they can breathe easy.

Without their cover they are naked – revealed as living hollow lives in service of mind control programming.

But nothing is by accident. The 'hollow man' state of consciousness has actually been cultivated to perfection in preparation for the culmination of decades, if not centuries, of mind control. However, before we address this in Chapter 11, where we reveal the future of the programs and the ultimate aim of those who designed them, let us take a moment in the following chapter to explore the most effective instrument of mind control programming ever devised: mainstream media.

Chapter 10

The Media Program

A television in every home. That was Motorola's promise to consumers in America in the early fifties. This new invention was, perhaps, the most brilliant mind control device ever conceived of, masquerading as the hottest thing in entertainment.

What a gift for the masses. Now, when you come home from work exhausted from your labors, you can zone out every night while watching the "programs" on your spanking new television set. And indeed, programs they were, cleverly designed to mind control the masses in three powerful ways – through direct brainwashing, through the addictive power of dopamine-producing sound and imagery and through the scheduled exhortations to buy, buy, buy, otherwise known as commercials. It was perfect, and thus began a new era in the mind control of the masses. Their thoughts and behavior could now be shaped in almost any desired way through their addiction to the box.

Celebrities had been held up to the masses long before the advent of television, but now, celebrity worship would become a veritable institution, for they would be used as the primary programmers of the masses on television, in film and in the news media – no matter it be about sex, wealth, politics, status, success, beauty and more.

Thus, celebrities became the gods of the culture, the standard of achievement, preternaturally perfect representations of the idealized human. The masses would predictably scramble to look like their idols, dress like their idols and behave like their idols. This fostered massive consumerism and the rise of designer brands.

Even if impoverished, the youth could be expected to find a way to compete with one another for the best designer shoes and jeans, and the rest could display their status in the culture or manipulate perception of their status with the expensive clothing and accessories of well-known designers. This would keep the people preoccupied with acquiring goods and finding ways to pay for these purchases in their never-ending quest for perceived superiority by becoming more like the culture's idols.

In addition to the institutionalization of celebrity came the falsification of news stories. Any event that dominated the news could powerfully program the masses for any purpose whatsoever: to feel hatred toward a common enemy, to sell off stocks, to prepare for war, to store goods, to live in a perpetual state of anxiety. All of this could be triggered at will by the words coming from the box news and its related sources – radio, magazines and newspapers.

During this time, it was important to have the world population believe the destruction of the planet was imminent through obsessive news coverage of the development and testing of nuclear bombs. With the use of them in Japan to end World War II, the nuclear bomb drills in schools, and the threatening news stories of nuclear build-up in enemy countries, it was easy to maintain the chronic vibration of fear, which was essential to obedience to the box and to the other programming institutions of the culture. Fear is an excellent, perhaps the best, motivator and thus was exploited to the fullest when programming of the population became an art form with the arrival of television.

Eventually, the TV set was not only in every home, but it was also in every room of every home. The addiction was complete. The pleasure value of shows caused the people to live for their moments in front of the television, to hunger and long for it, to dwell on the memory of it and to discuss it at work or with friends. With television in the bedroom of every child, the younger generation would receive its daily dose of brainwashing. With the youth the most vulnerable to mind control, each mind would be captured one by one through their favorite programs on the TV set.

Not only did the TV shows reflect the values the controllers wished to implant in the culture – values such as obedience to cultural norms of the era, I.Q. reduction through lowbrow comedy, greed and consumerism through quiz shows and advertising, and sublimated desire, anger and frustration through depictions of sex and violence – but the shows would also evolve as the controllers' agenda evolved to shape the desires, thoughts and beliefs of the viewers. Add to that the measurable passivity-inducing and brain-dulling effects of sitting for long periods in front of the tube, and the formula was better than perfect.

In the mix, were shows that popularized the worst behavior of human beings – fraud, theft, rape and murder. Eventually, the local news would become devoted to reporting crime stories as if they were the only important events of the day, their only competition being natural disasters, deadly diseases and other 'acts of God.'

The primetime news channels would take certain stories and run with them, portraying the incident and its consequences in devastating detail. Therefore, you not only saw endlessly repeated, graphic images of the disease, crime or event, both in real time and in its aftermath, but would also be subjected to a barrage of sanctimonious commentators and experts debating and reflecting on every aspect of the story ad infinitum.

Add to that the standard interviews of "first responders," of weeping relatives and friends of the victims, of witnesses of the crime, of curious passersby, of blanket-wrapped civilians who escaped unharmed, of local politicians looking to gain points with their constituency, of resourceful do-gooders providing rapidly organized help to survivors, not to mention the repeatedly flashed scenes of the event site itself and nearby environs, the distant footage of police cars, ambulances, trucks and/or police aimlessly walking around, the paramedics carting something (a body?) away on a stretcher, invariably a few words from a glazed-eyed, wounded participant, the inevitable celebrity appearance, a gaggle of news anchors, doctors, nurses and medical technicians moaning about absent medical treatments, tests or equipment when the need appears most urgent and the requisite interviews with desperately ill individuals deprived of that very life-saving service.

All of this would be brandished before the viewers who, mouths agape with shock, would absorb the ongoing horror from every angle. In this, you have a recipe for reaching most of the people most of the time with a story containing maximum surface believability and emotional pull.

Nothing would be left out when an event was being used for programming the masses. The viewer must be made to believe the horrific nature of the situation, its continuing threat to life and happiness and its anguishing affect on those most affected or close to the loved ones lost in the disaster.

News cameras would always be there, the all-seeing eye, conveniently filming even in heavily secured, potentially illegal locales such as hospital emergency rooms, intensive care units, operating rooms or jails, as well as adjacent to crackling wildfires, at the foot of lava-spewing volcanoes, or amidst flooding waters. No matter, as all of this, along with the many other improbabilities, would be accepted completely by brainwashed viewers.

News stations around the country, and even around the world, would harp on the same event, often showing the same stock footage, such that it seemed there were only one or two pictures of the event or of the victims aired over and over again.

The masses would inhale all of this agony and soldier on, their lives daily impacted by the misery news, yet somehow always needing to hear more. The feelings aroused were addictive, more so if it was shock, horror or grief. This would give rise to swelling hubris - something must be done! Each person would desperately try to think of a way, yet feel completely powerless to change the horror of the events. With hearts in mouths, they would listen for more and more information and watch every news channel they could to continually focus on the disaster and try to process the array of intense emotions being aroused.

As emotions peak, a has-been guitarist would surface to perform the perfect anthem on the primetime news, which would then become a radio hit, a group of children would assemble to recite a meaningful poem by someone who died in the destruction, a special exhibit of amateur paintings depicting the destruction would be filmed at a senior center.

All of this said to introduce the primary purpose of this sort of news programming. It is to install a bundle of specific beliefs via repeated trauma-based imagery and words, what from a higher perspective is known as a thought virus.

Once the virus has been released into the culture and continually re-energized with fanatical repetition and zeal, it is only a matter of time before the brainwashing is complete. The public believes the news and the stories and, therefore, through the repetition of imagery and words, virtually any belief can be installed and receive complete acceptance in the viewer's mind. The viewer may then be said to have been infected with a virus – and if the thought virus is, for example, about a health issue, some may believe so completely and feel so vulnerable, they will actually induce the appearance of this illness in their own body even to the point of dying on cue. That is the effect on the most vulnerable, the ones for whom there is little conscious resistance to the thought virus, perhaps because they are already old and sick, or perhaps because the force of the brainwash overwhelms their ability to maintain health. For a child or infant, their parents' beliefs outpicture in the child's health as children express the subconscious beliefs of the culture as embodied in the parents.

This is a world of illusion, illusion created by mind, driven by unconscious beliefs that are further reinforced by conscious beliefs. Conscious beliefs alone, however, are not enough to cause the thought virus to wreak havoc in one's body. One must impregnate the collective unconscious with a powerful belief, i.e., the thought virus, in order to drive what manifests in the surface reality.

The Media Program

What the masses do not know is that their world is an illusion created by mind and shaped by belief, both conscious and unconscious. Moreover, what the masses never knew was that the purpose of the television box – the news and all mainstream media – is to alter the conscious and unconscious mind in ways that serve the controllers. That means a diseased world can be created by powerfully installing beliefs in the conscious and unconscious mind.

What the masses cannot grasp or would find most difficult to accept is that most of the stories being pounded into their heads on the news and in paper/digital mediums are either pure theater or vast exaggerations of truth, no matter how apparently real, how visual, how visceral, how extensively and endlessly they are analyzed by eminent scientists and experts all over the world, or how well they are bemoaned by celebrity idols and well-known politicians.

The box was put into your home for one reason and one reason only – to control your thinking and behavior, i.e., shape it with installed beliefs and enlist your mind in willingly manifesting the agenda of the controllers as it evolves over time. If the viewer refuses to be trapped by the seemingly overwhelming agreement in the reports around the world and throughout their country, which appear to confirm the reality of an event, they would be able to see that it is all by design. They would understand that it is a coordinated psy-op or psychological operation on a global level, a form of psychological warfare with the purpose of taking over your mind and programming your mind. On seeing this, in knowing this, you are then protected to an extent from the programming.

Your safety lies in not participating in the programming by ending your addiction to the box and other forms of mainstream media. Though the programming will still reach you through your subconscious mind, which is inseparable from the collective, through the behavior and attitudes of those around you, and through your inability to escape the thought virus entirely by its very ubiquity, you will receive protection by recognizing, with the full power of your awareness as Infinite Being in a human encapsulation, that it is Not Real. You must stand in that realization though it may not be shared by anyone you know, though it may not be accepted by those with whom you attempt to share it, and though you may find yourself alone and isolated in your realization. You must stand in truth, as Truth is your savior. Quietly stand in truth and let the chips fall where they may. However, *you* shall not fall because you are able to see through the deception.

In the final chapter, we disclose the mainstream media's most bizarre harvest and the one most coveted by the controllers: the Transgender and Transhumanist Programs.

Chapter 11

The Transgender and Transhumanist Programs

O f all the programs, the most invisible ones are the most pernicious. And there we find the Transgender and Transhumanist Programs. These programs have entailed a prolonged period of preparation, so that in your current reality they unfold without raising a single eyebrow. Even if a few were to actually notice and put some pieces of the puzzle together, they would still remain hidden and invisible to the overwhelming majority who would view the awakening minds as insane. However, labeling something 'insane' simply means you can't under-stand it or, in this case, see it; for your heavily fogged and richly padded filter prevents the seeing of anything outside of your current range of beliefs.

Once a perspective has been expanded, usually through intensive exposure to new information, one marvels at their blindness when having been possessed by the previous perspective.

Overcoming cultural programming and ongoing mind control agendas is a matter of peeling an onion, each layer revealing an obvious truth or perception that was completely invisible to the same mind before that layer was peeled. In this way, an entire world population can remain squeezed into tight cultural filters for the entirety of civilized existence, and nothing need ever change other than what the programmers wish to introduce into the mix.

The human population is easily manipulated by mind control programming. As long as the status quo is maintained, the population will acquiesce because survival of the individual and of the family unit is its primary concerns. When an individual breaks formation with sightings of new land or, perhaps, has an extraordinary vision, they are quickly marginalized and isolated from the rest. In some primitive cultures, they would become the oracle, in others the new healer, while in modern society they are more likely to be ignored or hospitalized for psychosis.

Human beings literally cannot see what their filter will not allow and, therefore, will rationalize news of something they cannot see as madness, or minimize the discovery in some other way for the purpose of ensuring the continuation of their denial of truth. This truth, however, being another layer of the onion, must be confronted if greater awareness is to ever occur. Because the human locks in their perception in line with their filter, and automatically renders insignificant or nonexistent the sightings of one who peeled the next layer, they persist in affirming the certainty of their limited position.

Humans never fear ignorance, they fear being made fools of, even if keeping their head in the sand guarantees their ignorance of something they would do well to know as much about as possible.

The transgender and transhumanist agendas, which have already been rolled out and are "in your face," are two things of which the human would do well to make themself aware as soon as possible. But because humans are so averse to peeling the onion, the programmers have had a field day with those agendas, with no let up in sight.

What you ask is the transgender and transhumanist agendas? You may promise to listen to my answer, to hear with an open mind, yet it is certain you will find the programs too impossible to believe. Or perhaps you will accept information about one but reject it about the other. To accept both as already well-ensconced in your world is to defy belief, and, therefore, your mind recoils from that knowledge. That, or you allow your intellect to take over and acknowledge its possibility at a surface level, thereby protecting yourself from the shock of truth. For when this truth is registered, it does shock the human body/mind/spirit and naturally causes a storm of emotions.

The Transgender and Transhumanist Programs

Those who nod their head upon hearing these ideas have not heard anything and are as defended against the truth as the ones who would laugh in your face, or order you out of the room. All this said to prepare you for the transgender and transhumanist programming that is changing the nature of the human race as we speak.

So what is this mysterious agenda, you ask. Tell us already! Though I, The Bringer, will tell you what I feel able to share at this time, even that bit of truth will be scoffed at by the minds reading this who are encased in the narrow filter constructed out of the various programs afflicting human existence in your realm.

What if The Bringer, were to tell you that there is a concerted effort to, first gradually, and then with greater momentum, eliminate the human race as it now manifests, and replace it with highly controlled, self-replicating biological robots. The planning and execution leading to this result is a long one, spanning centuries. You are caught like deer in the headlights of an unprecedented experiment in race creation. The human is to be slowly relieved of gender definition and biological reproductive capabilities, i.e., rendered neutered and infertile, and in its place will be creatures similar to the one in that classic movie "RoboCop" – human-machine hybrids subject to total control by the programmers.

No more the diversity of messy human cultures, with their languages, quirks and skewed development requiring intense mind control programming to maintain the people's obliviousness to their origins as being sourced by the Divine. Imagine the many methods that needed to be introduced to manage this worldwide slave population, which not only includes the programs discussed in this book, and many more not discussed, but also an array of energy-based and food/environmental-based control methods to render the population weak and sickly. All of this in service of sustaining the separation from the truth of their being.

Though effective, it has been time-consuming and energy-intensive to persist in these means of controlling the population, which has been further exacerbated by the tendency for more individuals of higher vibrational bandwidth to attempt to awaken the deeply asleep masses. With efforts needing to be doubled and redoubled, the controllers decided to speed up the process of turning humans into virtual machines. This began somewhat obliquely with the normalization of gender fluidity in the media and the schools, and the inciting of gender identity conflict among the youth. It went on to include laws being enacted to remove gender from birth certificates, the sprouting of numerous gender identity clinics as if anticipating Black Friday crowds, the creation of gender-neutral bathrooms in schools and public places, the legal transfer of management of a child's gender identity from the home to the schools, and the passing out of hormonal blockers by the schools to preteen kids who are questioning their gender identity. Thus, the agenda went into high gear, and the transgender enforcers began a new phase of intensive transformation of the human race.

While these tactics will still take a few more decades to grip the world completely, the programmers are happy to play the long game, recognizing the infinite, eternal playing board upon which they move the pieces.

Along with The Transgender Program's medical, genetic and quantum redesign of the human being into infertile, androgynous beings, The Transhumanist Program requires an implanting of technological devices into this biological creature. At each stage of breaking them out, these implants will be presented as essential. Those who resist will find the implant connected to vital needs, such as accessing their bank accounts, paying bills or getting on an airplane. It will eventually seem as logical, necessary and normal for the people to receive implants as it now is to receive vaccines.

If you perform an analysis of what goes into vaccines, many disturbing truths emerge. Not only are unhealthy metals placed in vaccines in high levels, but other noxious chemicals and animal body parts are also mixed in, none of which have anything to do with protecting you from disease and everything to do with altering your DNA and serving up toxic metal loads. As part of the weakening of the population, vaccines have been extraordinarily effective while being sold by the medical establishment as critically important for health. It has even been made illegal for a parent to refuse them for their children. In the guise of protecting public health, all countries require certain vaccinations before allowing travelers into the country; another way in which vaccines are forced upon the public.

But the new world order will have a much neater, cleaner and more productive policy in place. They will take biological computers, i.e., human/machine hybrids, and make of them the slaves and servants of the elite across the world.

Transhumanism also involves merging human with animal DNA to create new creatures with special abilities and to enhance the pets that are so popular in the world today. Human and animal combinations, further augmented by robotic implants, will perform skilled labor of all kind as needed, based on their unique abilities. In this way, armies will be created in the lab as well as all manner of human hybrids, animal hybrids and designer pets.

Where does transgenderism fit in? In order to produce a state-controlled human machine or human/animal machine, a means of destroying long-accepted ideas of what a human being is, including ideas about gender and, ultimately, human reproduction, must first be put in place: Blur the lines between how the genders dress and behave, encourage and normalize childhood questioning of gender identity, legally hand out hormone blockers to prepubescent children in the schools without needing their parents' permission, increase infertility in the general public, have men and women share bathrooms, allow individuals to use the public bathroom of their preferred gender identity even if their physical genitalia is of the opposite sex thereby ignoring potential risk for women and children, make any written or verbalized expressions of concern, or any inquiry regarding the transgender agenda to be demonized as politically incorrect in a world where anything deemed 'politically incorrect' has been programmed to automatically trigger intense reactivity in the brainwashed masses.

What of this business of hiding in plain sight, you ask? The hardest thing for the average person to accept is that the individuals whose faces are always in the media and/who grace the television screen, the movie screen, perform music or serve other prominent roles in the culture, including politicians, sports figures, news anchors, royals, top executives, models, actors, actresses and entertainers, are in large number reversed to their natural gender. The gender reversal phenomenon is further intergenerational and extends to their children and beyond.

Some families already use in utero genetic/hormonal procedures to make of the child a hybrid creation gender-wise and to add certain gifts and abilities. If one wishes to be in the public eye, these agendas must be served according to one's lineage, and this may include surgery, gender dissemblance or other agenda-forwarding activities of that persona in the culture. In many cases, the individual is opposite the gender they appear to be or has been literally redesigned in the lab to be a streamlined blend of male and female, and are able to choose their presenting gender.

Accept this or not, it is fact and a fact that stands before your eyes day in and day out – that male actor you adore may well be a female with surgical and hormonal enhancements, or that beautiful female model actually a hormonally and surgically altered male. Whenever you look at images in the media, watch a movie or TV show, or go on the internet, you are being inundated with images of celebrities; always the same faces over and over again. You have been made to feel that these people are extraordinary by the constant focus on their supposed attributes, status and accomplishments. If it weren't so, surely they wouldn't be in the public eye and thereby deemed worthy of your idolatry.

You are programmed to idolize them with their apparent beauty, wealth, talent and power, to desire them sexually, to desire to emulate them. Yet their entire persona has been scientifically constructed with the further assistance of expert make-up, hair, wigs and clothing, to make you forget normal male and female anatomy, to make you oblivious to the fact that your idol's gender has been reversed. What you desire and admire in what you may think is a celebrity of the opposite sex may actually be someone who is the same gender as you. That this subterfuge creates warping of the subconscious of the adoring public while the public remains oblivious and resistant to truth, and continues to worship their celebrity idols, is proof of the power of this chronic, prolonged deception which has been perpetrated on the people.

Who are you really being programmed to fantasize about sexually or emulate in your own appearance, fashion and behavior, but individuals of reversed gender. This programming is presently in full force to blur and merge concepts of masculinity and femininity in order to install the reconfigured/neutered male and female as the normal masculine and feminine, thus preparing you for the gradual elimination of the genders and the rise of the machine.

For more information on the transgender agenda from a higher consciousness perspective, please see book four in the Real Enlightenment series by S, F. Howe, entitled *Transgender America: Spirit, Identity and the Emergence of the Third Gender*.

In Conclusion

The Face of Freedom

What would a free human look like you may wonder, after reading this litany of means by which you are inexorably diverted from True Being. Go to a mirror and look at yourself. That is the face of freedom. It is a human, becoming. But how, you ask, can I rid myself of the mind control programming that has ruled my life from my first breath? The short answer: You cannot. It is rooted in your being, it permeates your subconscious, it clogs the invisible highways of consciousness.

Scarcity and all the systems it spews forth are deeply entrenched in your culture. Your role is to see reality and to know the truth while living the most authentic life available to you. Your goal is no longer to pursue the carrots held out by the controllers but to quietly ask your higher self as often as you need to, 'What wants to happen next?' By bringing yourself into harmony with your true self, while eschewing the conformity performance expected by society, you step closer to fulfilling your potential. You do this knowing it is a process, as seeing what is potential for you evolves the further you remove yourself from the prescribed course.

The natural process of maturation throughout a lifetime also offers opportunity for reinventing yourself, as the decisions of youth, not to mention the decisions arising from the early zeal of a spiritual awakening, evolve through the tempering of time. Your entire approach to life must shift toward the experimental. Relinquishing the programming that sets you on a course to prove your worth through accepted cornerstones of accomplishment, leaves you free to explore what truly compels you. Avoiding or limiting the immobilizing four-square of family, home, school and career allows you to control your time more effectively.

In recognizing that all of you have prior commitments, such as raising children, supporting yourself and/or your family, paying mortgages or school tuition, etc., rest assured that this is not an invitation to abandon everything, most especially your ongoing familial or financial responsibilities, and start over. Instead, begin where you are. You need change nothing but your own perspective on the people, things, and experiences you have accumulated and which you call 'your life.' The yeast of understanding has enormous transformational power and will guide your future decisions.

If you have been moved to read this book through to this end point, you may now know that your freedom is certain. If it appears impossible, it is because the all-pervasive forces that directed your path to where you are now persist and demand obedience. But just stepping away from the compulsion to follow the sirens of mind control, those endless trigger phrases and images in the media, the ubiquitous false beliefs espoused in the culture, invites a higher vibration. When your frequency rises through the objective awareness of 'what is,' your entire reality transforms, not unlike changing the channel on your television set.

There is a reason you are in this particular world, with all of its restrictions and limitations. You are here to push against the limits of your programming, to know the truth of who you are, to crack the shell that encases you, to peck your way out bit by bit until, matted with moisture and exhaustion, you shake out your feathers and take your first deep breath of fresh air.

Who are you? What will you become? When you seek to be a transparency for the highest in you, the answer may surprise, but will also delight. Your highest vibrational truth is always the most joyful and freeing.

Before you go, don't forget to download your free gift, "How to Deconstruct a Troublesome Situation." This bonus report will help you find greater peace and emotional freedom while navigating the ups and downs of everyday life.

To get your bonus gift, go to:
https://bit.ly/DeconstructSituation/

Did You Enjoy This Book?

Dear Reader,

Thank you for reading *The Bringer Discourses: On Waking Up to the Mind Control Programs of the Matrix Reality.* I hope you enjoyed this book.

My purpose in writing this book is to reveal the hidden programming within everyday life in order to help awaken and support those seeking emotional and psychological freedom.

If you would like to help me reach more readers with this book, nothing would help more than your writing a brief review on Amazon. It would mean the world to me, and I'd love to read your review!

Wishing you the very best,

S. F. Howe

Books by S. F. Howe

MIND · BODY · SPIRIT

HIGHER CONSCIOUSNESS

Matrix Man: How To Become Enlightened, Happy And Free In An Illusion World

The author reveals a new reality paradigm that will liberate you from the limiting beliefs and cultural programming that prevent a joyful and fulfilling life. Available in print and digital editions.

The Top Ten Myths Of Enlightenment: Exposing The Truth About Spiritual Enlightenment That Will Set You Free!

Essential reading for spiritual seekers. What no one else will tell you to help you avoid the pitfalls of the spiritual journey. Available in print and digital editions.

The Bringer Discourses: On Waking Up To The Mind Control Programs Of The Matrix Reality

For those seeking freedom from cultural indoctrination, these channeled teachings offer a higher dimensional perspective on the most ingrained and unquestioned aspects of everyday life, and have the ability to heal and awaken humanity. Available in print and digital editions.

PLANT INTELLIGENCE

Secrets Of The Plant Whisperer: How To Care For, Connect, And Communicate With Your House Plants

A plant whisperer reveals the hidden truth about plants and why relating to them in a conscious way is vital for their health and well-being. Available in print and digital editions.

PERSONAL GROWTH

Vision Board Success: How To Get Everything You Want With Vision Boards!

A powerful technique for achieving your goals and manifesting your desires. Available in print and digital editions.

Sex Yoga: The 7 Easy Steps To A Mind-Blowing Kundalini Awakening! i

A technique for activating the chakras to induce a powerful kundalini experience. Available in print and digital editions.

Morning Routine For Night Owls: How To Supercharge Your Day With A Gentle Yet Powerful Morning Routine!

Morning rituals aren't only for morning people, and they don't have to be rough and tumble or performed at top speed to set up a perfect day. Welcome to the world of the gentle yet powerful wake-up routine for night owls! Available in print and digital editions.

CONSCIOUS HEALTH

Transgender America: Spirit, Identity And The Emergence Of The Third Gender

A higher consciousness perspective on the Transgender Agenda; what it is and why it is being rolled out at breakneck speed to social engineer a gender dysphoria epidemic. Available in print and digital editions.

When Nothing Else Works: How To Cure Your Lower Back Pain Fast!

The simple method that no doctor will ever tell you about. Requires no drugs, no surgery, and no special equipment. Available in print and digital editions.

About the Author

S. F. Howe is a transformational psychologist and noted contributor to the body/mind/spirit literature for books and teachings on the subjects of higher consciousness, personal growth, conscious health and plant intelligence.

Howe began teaching at the university level while a doctoral candidate in clinical psychology, and went on to work in hospitals and clinics for more than 25 years as a psychotherapist, staff psychologist, clinical program consultant and director of chemical dependency and psychiatric programs.

In the midst of graduate studies, a profound spiritual awakening led to a complete reevaluation of the author's life path. Thus began a spiritual journey along the road less traveled, extending far beyond clinical psychology, conventional reality paradigms and both traditional religion and new age spirituality.

While engaged in a unique, ongoing process of discovery, the author enjoys sharing an ever-expanding understanding of the true nature of reality. Howe's primary intention is to bring an end to suffering by guiding others on a well-worn path to truth and expanded awareness.

Many of those who have experienced Howe's input and presence report emotional and physical healing, life-changing realizations and dramatic personal transformation.

S. F. Howe may be contacted for speaking and teaching engagements. Please direct all inquiries to info@diamondstarpress.com.

Free Gift

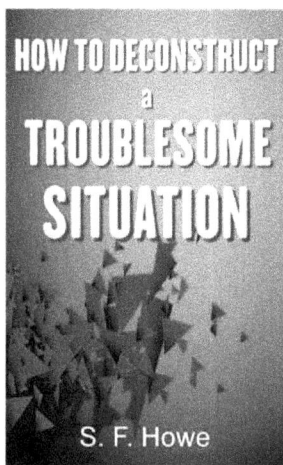

As our thanks to you for reading *The Bringer Discourses: On Waking Up to the Mind Control Programs of the Matrix Reality*, we would like you to download the bonus report, "How to Deconstruct a Troublesome Situation." Inside this report is a powerful technique that will help you strip any problem down to its core and give you the objectivity needed to find the best solution.

To get your bonus gift, go to:
https://bit.ly/DeconstructSituation/